THEN & NOW

ARMS *and* ARMOR

Written by Adrian Gilbert
Illustrated by James Field

COPPER BEECH BOOKS
BROOKFIELD, CONNECTICUT

© Aladdin Books Ltd
1997
© U.S. text 1997
Designed and produced by
Aladdin Books Ltd
28 Percy Street
London W1P 0LD

First published in the
United States in 1997 by
Copper Beech Books,
an imprint of
The Millbrook Press
2 Old New Milford Road
Brookfield
Connecticut 06804

Editor
Simon Beecroft
Design
David West Children's
Book Design
Designer
Robert Perry
Picture Research
Brooks Krikler Research
Illustrator
James Field –
Simon Girling &
Associates

Printed in Belgium

Library of Congress
Cataloging-in-Publication Data
Gilbert, Adrian.
Arms and armor / Adrian
Gilbert ; illustrated by James
Field.
p. cm. — (Then and now)
Includes index.
ISBN 0-7613-0605-6
(lib. bdg.)
1. Weapons—History—
Juvenile literature. 2. Armor–
–History—Juvenile literature.
I. Field, James. 1959- .
II. Title. III. Series: Then &
now (Brookfield, Conn.)
U800.G47 1997   97-10019
623.4—dc21   CIP

CONTENTS

INTRODUCTION   3

BOWS AND ARROWS   4
SWORDS AND DAGGERS   6
STAFF WEAPONS   8
BODY ARMOR   10
MUSKETS AND RIFLES   12
PISTOLS AND REVOLVERS   14
MACHINE GUNS   16
MORTARS AND GRENADES   18
BOOBY TRAPS AND MINES   19
FIELD ARTILLERY   20
THE BIG GUNS   22
ARMORED VEHICLES   24
MISSILES AND ROCKETS   26
SECRET WEAPONS   28

GLOSSARY   30
INDEX   32

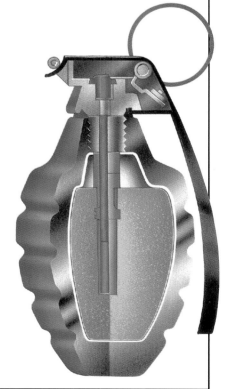

INTRODUCTION

The earliest weapons are thought to have been flint axes used by Stone Age people 250,000 years ago. Since then, arms and armor have played an important role in human history. This book traces the development of weapons, from simple axes and bows to today's assault rifles and battle tanks.

The history of arms and armor has always depended on technological development. The great breakthrough came with the Industrial Revolution in the 18th century, when metals such as steel were first manufactured in large quantities. As a result, weapons became increasingly effective and deadly. But as arms improved, opposing forces were compelled to develop better protection and more sophisticated weapons.

The constant attempts to outwit an enemy have seen the manufacture of an enormous range of weapons, many of which have been rapidly overtaken by improved designs. This has led to some surprising results, such as the return of earlier weapons and defenses, including the crossbow and body armor.

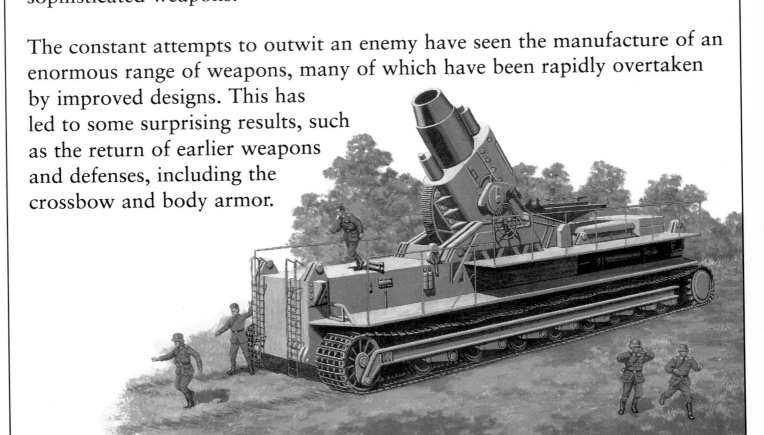

BOWS AND ARROWS

Bows were first used for hunting during the Stone Age, 250,000 years ago. The ancient Egyptians were the first people to use bows and arrows in warfare, in about 5000 B.C. Until the introduction of firearms in the 16th century, archers played a crucial role in combat. Bows were made from tough, flexible wood like yew. The equipment used in modern archery is derived from the shapes and qualities of medieval long bows.

EARLY ARCHERS
Stone Age people used arrows with flint arrowheads *(above)* to hunt large or fast-moving animals. The arrowheads, carved from pieces of solid rock, were deadly sharp.

ANCIENT WARFARE
The ancient Egyptians fought many battles against neighboring peoples, including the fierce Assyrians *(left)*, in which both sides were armed with bows and arrows. The Assyrian Army, which was well-organized and its soldiers well-trained, eventually conquered the mighty Egyptian Empire.

MEDIEVAL ARCHERS

In the Middle Ages, bows were used by archers in the Norman army to help defeat the English at the Battle of Hastings in 1066 *(right)*. During the late Middle

Ages (14th and 15th centuries A.D.), English archers used a more effective bow, the longbow *(left)*, to win several battles against the French – including Agincourt in 1415. Arrows from longbows could pierce plate armor at over 109 yards (300 feet), but using one took years of practice.

ROBIN HOOD
According to legend, Robin Hood was an outlaw who lived in Sherwood Forest, England, during the 12th century. He used his great skill with a bow and arrow to defend the poor against a corrupt sheriff.

ARROWHEADS

An arrow is made up of a wooden or steel shaft, with feathers or flights at one end (to make it fly straight) and an arrowhead (*right*) at the other. Hunting arrowheads often have barbs along the side, which catch in the animal. Bodkins are arrows designed to pierce steel plate.

General-purpose

Bodkin

Japanese

African (with barbs)

Indian

COMPETITION BOWS
Today's bows (*left*) are made from artificial materials such as fiberglass, which is glued together in strips.
They are very accurate and are used in sporting competitions, including the Olympic Games.

CROSSBOWS

The crossbow is a powerful and accurate bow, first used in the Middle Ages. Often the archer had to use a mechanical winding device to pull back the string (*above*). Crossbows are still used by troops today. This soldier (*below*) practices using one while wearing night-vision glasses.

HUNTING BUFFALO
Native American tribes used wooden bows to hunt buffalo (*above*). They rode alongside the animals, so they could shoot them at short range. Buffalo provided them with food and with leather for quivers (*left*), which held arrows, as well as clothes and tents.

SWORDS AND DAGGERS

The earliest swords were made from bronze (*left*) and date back to at least 2000 B.C. The two main functions of swords are cutting and thrusting, although there are many different types. Daggers and knives are short thrusting weapons used in hand-to-hand combat. Swords today are used for ceremonial purposes, but bayonets (*see page 7*) are still used by soldiers in battle.

THE RIGHT SWORD FOR THE JOB

The Romans (*right*) were armed with a short sword called a gladius, which was used for thrusting at the enemy from short range. During the Middle Ages, swords became longer and, in the 16th century, some swords had become so heavy that they had to be held with both hands (*right*). Cavalrymen, who fought on horseback, needed a single-edged sword, which could be used for thrusting and cutting. French cavalrymen (*left*) in the Napoleonic Wars (1793-1815) carried swords with slightly curved blades called sabers.

SWORDS OF THE SAMURAI

Japanese samurai warriors used some of the finest (and sharpest!) swords ever produced (*above*). The blades were made by covering a soft iron core with layers of steel. A dagger and a skewer (*below*) were carried on either side of the scabbard. The best swords were handed down from generation to generation, and could last many hundreds of years.

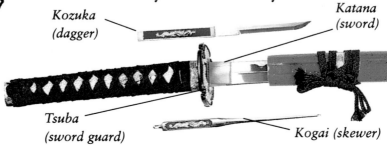

Kozuka (dagger)

Katana (sword)

Tsuba (sword guard)

Kogai (skewer)

ON GUARD!

In the 16th century, long, narrow, extremely sharp swords, called rapiers, were developed. These, and several variants, were used by wealthy people to defend themselves, and for use in prearranged sword fights called duels (*below*). Dueling has now been replaced by the sport of fencing.

Bars for gripping

Le Petit Journal
LE DUEL HENRY-PICQUART

BLADES FROM INDIA AND NEPAL

Daggers and knives come in all shapes and sizes. The famous kukri knife carried by the Gurkha soldiers of Nepal (*above*) can slice off a man's head with a single thrust! The Indian kataar (*left*), unlike most European daggers, is gripped by two bars so that the vertical metal rods support the wrist. It is used in a punching action.

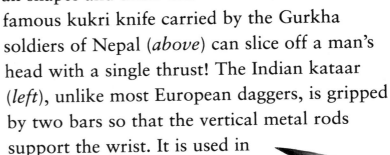

Plug bayonet

BAYONETS

Bayonets (*right*) are blades fixed to the ends of muskets or rifles. The first plug bayonets of the late 17th century fitted directly into the muzzle and had to be taken out to fire the musket. Later, they were fitted to the side of the barrel and, by the 19th century, long sword bayonets were common. Bayonets are still used today, but they are much shorter.

Sword bayonet

Modern bayonet

SHORTER BLADES

Daggers and knives are shorter, lighter, and handier than swords, but they can still be lethal. The Aztec people of Mexico used ceremonial knives (*above left*) made of stone (either flint or obsidian) in sacrificial rituals. Modern soldiers are equipped with combat knifes – although they often use them just for cutting up food!

MAGICAL SWORDS

The Viking Norsemen, warriors from northern Europe, treasured their swords very highly and some believed they had magical powers. Viking warriors gave their swords names, like "widow maker" or "fire of Odin."

COLONEL JIM BOWIE (1796-1836)

James "Jim" Bowie was a famous American frontiersman and soldier who invented a knife (left), which bears his name. The knife had a heavy, upturned blade, which was found to be good in hand-to-hand fighting. He was killed fighting the Mexicans at the battle of the Alamo.

Lacquered wooden scabbard

STAFF WEAPONS

Stone Age people found that the effectiveness of a weapon was increased by attaching it to a pole, or staff. Staff weapons gave the warrior greater reach and more power. They range from ball-and-chain flails (*right*) to long-handled thrusting weapons like pikes (*see page 9*). During the Middle Ages, staff weapons were widely used, and police forces today continue to use them in the form of clubs and nightsticks.

PREHISTORIC AXES

Stone Age warriors fashioned simple ax heads (*above*) from pieces of flint. The earliest axes were held in the hand, but later they were tied onto short staffs.

WAR HAMMERS

These heavy weapons were used by ancient peoples such as the Hittites (*left*), who lived in the area that is now Turkey. In the Middle Ages, war hammers were designed not so much to penetrate armor but to break bones and damage the man beneath the armor.

DEADLY CLUBS

Some of the simpler types of staff weapons, clubs are used to batter an opponent by sheer weight and force. During the Middle Ages, knights would sometimes carry a short club called a mace (*below left*), which was made of steel and could crush someone's head. During World War I, soldiers used homemade clubs, which they used in nighttime trench raids when they needed to be silent (*right*).

Mace

South Sea Islands club

MARTIAL ARTS

Nunchakus, or articulated rice flails (*above*), are used in Japanese martial arts. These farming tools were used as improvised weapons at a time when martial arts were banned. Many martial arts, such as judo and karate, are based on combat without weapons.

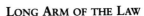

LONG ARM OF THE LAW

Police have been armed with short wooden batons, called truncheons (*left*), since the 1820s. Metal and rubber truncheons are also used today, and many have side handles for greater control (*below*).

Bronze Age axhead

A CUTTING EDGE

Axes have heavy blades (*above*) fitted to short staffs. They are not as maneuverable as swords, but they have great force and can cut through chain mail and plate armor (*see pages 10-11*). Many differently shaped blades are found on axes used by warriors around the world (*left*).

PIKES AND HALBERDS

During the Middle Ages, foot soldiers needed to protect themselves from mounted knights, and they did this by holding them off with very long staff weapons. Pikes (*below*) had simple spearheads and could be 18 feet (5.5 meters) long, while halberds had ax heads as well as spear points.

AN IMPENETRABLE WALL

Using pikes, rows of soldiers formed a thick barrier to advancing enemy troops. Soldiers farther back could also reach forward to attack the enemy with these long weapons.

Tomahawk

African ax

English battle-ax

Chinese ax

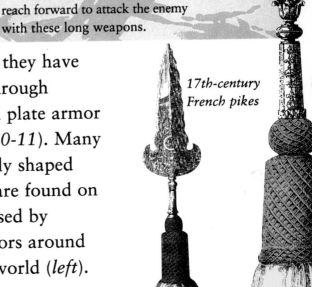

17th-century French pikes

BODY ARMOR

Armor protects soldiers from enemy weapons. The Greeks and Romans used it extensively, but the development of armor reached its peak during the Middle Ages. With the development of firearms that could penetrate metal, most soldiers stopped wearing armor, although cavalrymen still wore helmets and breastplates until the 19th century. Recently, new types of body armor have been introduced for soldiers and specialist police on riot duty (*below right*).

HOPLITE HELMETS
Greek infantrymen, called hoplites, wore heavy armor and large helmets, which were made from bronze and had a brightly colored horsehair crest. This Corinthian-type helmet (*above*) covered the entire face, so that only the eyes and mouth were exposed.

ROMAN PROTECTION
Many Roman soldiers wore breastplates (*left*). Another type of Roman armor, worn by legionaries in the first to the third centuries A.D., was made up of strips of metal held together by leather straps on the inside. This made it light and flexible.

FROM MAIL TO PLATE

Chain mail armor was made from many iron rings linked together (*below*). Soldiers wearing it could move around quite easily, but it provided only limited protection from arrows, heavy swords, and axes. During the Middle Ages, knights (*above*) began to add pieces of plate armor until, eventually, they wore complete suits of plate armor. These were skillfully made and were not as heavy and cumbersome as they look (*right*).

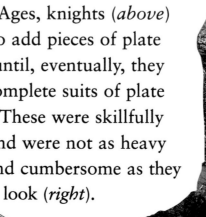

ARMOR FROM JAPAN

Samurai warriors wore armor made from iron and leather (*right*). The armor was usually coated in black lacquer, which prevented the iron from rusting. High-ranking samurai had armor decorated with brass and sometimes even gold. The helmet, or kabuto, had a wide protective neck guard.

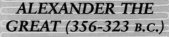

FROM CIVIL WAR TO WORLD WAR I

During the English Civil War (1642-1646), cavalrymen (*below left*) wore "lobster pot" helmets as well as breast and backplates, underneath which were thick leather coats. After the Civil War, armor began to die out, but during World War I (1914-1918) bulletproof armor was introduced. It was very heavy and was only worn by a few troops on guard duty (*right*).

ARMOR FOR TODAY
Modern armor can be made from a new material called Kevlar. This is made of layers of synthetic fibers and is stronger than steel, but is flexible and light (*right*). Different types of Kevlar protect against knives or bullets.

Layers of synthetic fabric

Fabric or plastic cover

WEIGHT PROBLEMS?
It has been said that some medieval armor was so heavy that riders had to be lifted onto their saddles using a mechanical hoist. In fact, full body armor weighed no more than about 44 lb (20 kg).

MUSKETS AND RIFLES

The earliest effective muskets – known as matchlocks – fired solid-lead bullets. They were inaccurate and slow to load. During the 19th century, muskets were replaced by rifles, in which spiraled grooves (rifling) were cut into the barrel that caused the bullet to spin, making it more accurate. A skilled marksman could hit a target at ranges of over 1,000 yards (3,000 feet). The development of breech-loading rifles allowed faster reloading and firing (*see page 13*).

LIGHT A FIRE
Matchlocks were so-called because the musketeer (*right*) had to use a smoldering piece of cord or match to light the priming pan, which fired the gun. To load the gun, the musketeer poured gunpowder from his powder flask (*above*) down the muzzle of the barrel, followed by the bullet and some cloth or paper to hold it all in place.

POWDER AND SHOT
Shotguns (*below*), unlike muskets or rifles, do not normally fire single bullets, but shoot many small pellets, or shot. Shotguns were developed in the 19th century for hunting small, fast-moving animals like rabbits and birds. Recently, soldiers have started using modern pump-action shotguns for fighting indoors and in other confined spaces.

19th-century Purdey shotgun

Pump-action shotgun

GUN THAT WON THE WEST!

The Winchester rifle was favored by cowboys (*right*) because it was light and accurate. It allowed up to 15 cartridges to be inserted into a tubular magazine that ran below the barrel. As each shot was fired, a lever, or bolt, was pulled back to eject the empty case, and pushed forward to bring a new cartridge forward.

Telescopic sight

AMMUNITION

During the 19th century, the lead balls fired from muskets and rifles (*above right*) were replaced by cartridges (*left*), which consisted of a brass case containing the charge and a bullet. Some cartridges have armor-piercing bullets, which are made from hardened steel and can cut through armor plate.

ASSAULT RIFLE
Assault rifles are fully automatic weapons. The M16 (*below*) was used extensively by U.S. troops in Vietnam. The modern Austrian-built 5.56mm Steyr AUG (*above*) can fire a magazine of up to 30 bullets in a few seconds, or can fire single shots.

ORIGINS
The first reference to a "hand gonne" (as it was called) appeared in a manuscript as early as 1364. This gun was a small, iron tube tied to a piece of wood, which fired lead balls. But it was not until the early 16th century that handguns were used by foot soldiers in battle.

MODERN RIFLES

By 1900 the old muzzle-loading, single-shot firearms (*below*) had been replaced by breech-loading rifles, such as the British .303 Lee Enfield. It was fitted with a magazine, which allowed up to ten shots to be fired. During the 1980s, the British Army began to use the SA 80 assault rifle, which has a 30-round magazine and can be fitted with a telescopic sight. Snipers use the .50 Barrett M82A1, which fires armor-piercing bullets accurately to ranges of over 2,000 yards (6,000 feet).

ANNIE OAKLEY
(1860-1926)

Famous in the "Wild" West, Annie Oakley made a living as a crack shot. She could shoot a bullet through the spots on a playing card thrown into the air, and put out a candle by shooting a bullet through the flame!

U.S. 19th-century single-shot rifle

.303 Lee Enfield

SA 80 assault rifle

.50 Barrett M82A1

13

PISTOLS AND REVOLVERS

Pistols are much easier to handle than muskets and were used by officers, cavalrymen, highwaymen, and gentlemen in duels. Early pistols, called wheel locks, were replaced in the 17th century by flintlocks, which were cheaper and more reliable. During the 19th century, inventors began to design handguns that would fire several shots before the cylinder needed reloading. The first of these multi-shot weapons was the revolver, followed by the automatic pistol.

Cock

Trigger

FLINTLOCKS

To fire a flintlock pistol (*above*), the spring-mounted cock was drawn back. When the trigger was pulled, the cock was released and would hit the steel striking plate (*below*), producing sparks which ignited the gunpowder.

WILD WEST WEAPONS

The expansion of the American West in the 19th century coincided with the development of many new weapons, including breech-loading rifles (*see page 12*) and revolvers, such as the Colt .45 (*see page 15*), which were used by everyone, from cowboys (*above*) to soldiers, settlers, and Native Americans.

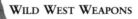

CRACK SHOTS

In the late 18th century, flintlock pistols began to replace swords as the main dueling weapon (*above*). Dueling pistols were always made in pairs and were of the highest quality to ensure accuracy. Today, the military and police practice accurate shooting at target ranges using modern pistols (*above right*).

HISTORICAL DUELS
Many important people took part in duels, including the Duke of Wellington, who defeated Napoléon at the Battle of Waterloo in 1815, and Lord Castlereagh, who became British foreign secretary in 1812. The famous Russian writer Aleksandr Pushkin was killed in a duel in 1837.

REVOLVING CYLINDERS

Colt .45

During the 1830s and 1840s, several inventors began to develop handguns with cylinders containing five or six cartridges.
The cylinder revolved so that the cartridges could be fired one at a time up the barrel. Only when the last cartridge was fired would the cylinder have to be reloaded. Colt (*left*) and Remington (*above*) were two of the most famous makes of the new handgun – called a revolver – which replaced the single-shot pistol and the slow, unreliable pepperbox pistol (*right*).

Remington

SAMUEL COLT
(1814-1862)
Colt was an American inventor and gunmaker who carved an early version of a revolver out of wood. He produced the first working revolver in 1835, and introduced a system of mass production for the weapon.

Pepperbox

THE LUGER PISTOL
Developed in the early 20th century, the distinctive-looking Luger pistol was adopted by the German Army and used in World War I and World War II (*left*). It could fire eight bullets in succession, from a magazine stored in the handgrip.

MODERN WEAPONS

The Israeli Desert Eagle (*above*) is a large, powerful, semi-automatic pistol, which uses a propellant gas to reload each time the trigger is pulled. Revolvers, too, are still widely used by armies and police forces: The highly powerful and exceptionally heavy .44in Magnum is perhaps the most famous since its use by the actor Clint Eastwood in the *Dirty Harry* movies (*right*).

MACHINE GUNS

The machine gun is one of the most fearsome weapons used by soldiers. Some machine guns can fire more than a thousand shots per minute. The first effective machine guns were developed in the late 19th century, and during World War I (1914-1918) they proved to be battle winners. There are many different types, but they all work on the principle of rapid and fully automatic fire. This means the soldier only has to cock the gun and hold down the trigger: Bullets will fire continuously as ammunition is fed into it from a cloth or metal belt, or from a magazine.

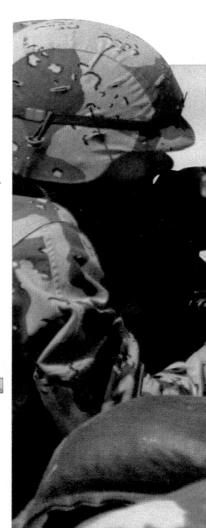

A PROTOTYPE
An early attempt to design a machine gun was made by James Puckle in 1717 (*above*). In trials, the gun fired up to nine shots every minute, but the British Army was not impressed and it was soon forgotten.

THE GATLING GUN
A hand-cranked machine gun (*left*) was invented by James Gatling and was used during the U.S. Civil War (1861-1865). The gun had several barrels, which revolved around a central axis. It was one of the most successful early machine guns.

TOWARD WORLD WAR I

In 1884, Hiram Maxim developed a portable machine gun, which used the recoil of the bullet to reload each cartridge. By 1914, most world powers, including the United States, had adopted the Maxim gun. Another type of machine gun, called the Hotchkiss, worked on a different principle: Its cartridges were reloaded by escaping gas. This Hotchkiss gun (*left*) was operated by Indian soldiers in World War I.

HIRAM MAXIM (1840-1916)
Born in Maine, Maxim settled in Britain, where he invented his machine gun. He also developed a smokeless form of gunpowder called "maximite." He was knighted in Britain, in 1901 for his inventions.

Bren gun

WORLD WAR II

The German Army used the MG 34 machine gun (*below*) during World War II. This air-cooled weapon was reasonably light and accurate with a high rate of fire. The British and Americans were impressed with the MG 34 and after the war they copied the German concept to produce what are now called general purpose machine guns (GPMGs). The British-made Bren gun (*above*) was also used during the war, and it was considered a highly effective light machine gun (LMG).

MG 34

TOMMY GUNS

Standard machine guns fire heavy bullets, but after World War I inventors began to use light pistol bullets in a fully automatic weapon. They became known as submachine-guns (SMGs) and were easy to use and carry. One of the first designs was the Thompson, nicknamed the tommy gun and used by American gangsters in the 1920s (*right*).

IN THE AIR

During World War I, machine guns were strapped onto aircraft (*above*). Later "interruptor devices" were used to synchronize the guns to fire in between the blades of the propellers. Machine guns have been fitted to many types of aircraft, including helicopter gunships used during the Vietnam War (*below*).

MODERN MACHINE GUNS

During the Vietnam conflict (1965-1975) and the 1991 war in the Gulf, U.S. troops were armed with the 7.62mm M60 GPMG. Every squad of ten to twelve infantrymen was equipped with an M60, which, because of its weight, was given to the strongest man to carry. The soldiers nicknamed it "the Hog!"

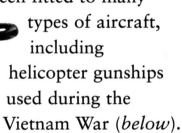

TODAY'S SMGs

The Israeli Uzi (*below*) is a compact, modern submachine-gun. This weapon weighs very little and is suited for close combat and combat indoors as it is not highly accurate.

MORTARS AND GRENADES

The earliest mortars, such as this late 18th-century, Indian-made "tiger" mortar (*right*), were very heavy. Today's mortars are a special form of lightweight artillery used by the infantry. Mortars have steep angles of fire, so that explosive charges are lobbed high into the air before falling onto the target. The infantry also use grenades for hand-to-hand combat.

IN THE TRENCHES
The modern type of mortars was developed during World War I (*above*). With a longer range than the hand-thrown grenade, they could drop a high-explosive shell directly into the enemy's trenches. They were also light enough to be carried around.

MODERN MORTARS
Modern mortars, such as this one being deployed by NATO soldiers in the Bosnian War (1992-1995, *left*), are accurate and powerful. An average infantry mortar can fire a shell at least 5,500 yds (16,500 ft).

GRENADE LAUNCHERS
In the 16th century, hand-held grenade launchers were developed to increase the range of the grenade. The fuse had to be lit very carefully to avoid a potentially fatal injury to the grenadier.

PULL OUT THE PIN

The earliest examples of grenades are medieval, such as this Arabic one made of clay (*left*). Grenades were used extensively in World War I (*below left*). Often, grenades were made from old cans filled with explosives and nails! In a modern grenade (*right*), the pin is pulled out to release the safety lever and prime the detonator. After a few seconds, the main charge explodes, shattering the case into lethal pieces.

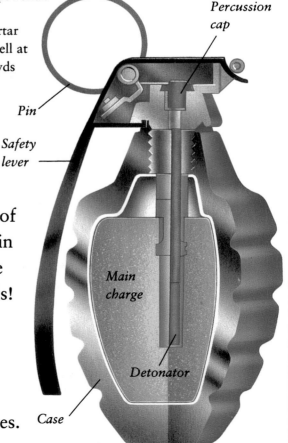

Percussion cap

Pin

Safety lever

Main charge

Detonator

Case

BOOBY TRAPS AND MINES

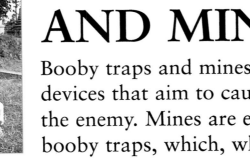

Booby traps and mines are hidden devices that aim to cause damage to the enemy. Mines are explosive booby traps, which, when buried in the ground, are very hard to find. Special troops are trained to use metal detectors (*above right*), to locate mines.

CIVILIAN DAMAGE
A major problem with hidden mines is that they can be accidentally detonated long after a war is over. In places like Cambodia, millions of mines have been left in the ground and ordinary farmers end up stepping on them – with tragic results (*above*).

Pressure switch

Main charge

ANTITANK MINES
Constructed to blow up armored vehicles, antitank mines (*above*) are buried a few inches under the ground. They are fitted with a pressure switch, which will only detonate the mine when a heavy vehicle, such as a tank, goes over it. It is unlikely that a person walking over one would set it off.

Trip prong

Main charge

ANTIPERSONNEL MINES
Smaller than antitank mines, antipersonnel mines (*left*) go off when a person's foot is placed on them. The intention is to maim, not kill, because the enemy country will then have to pay for expensive hospital treatment.

BOOBY TRAPS IN VIETNAM

The Viet Cong, who fought American soldiers in the Vietnam War (1965-1975), were not as well armed and equipped as the Americans. But they used their extensive knowledge of the

jungle terrain to plant booby traps to catch American patrols. They stretched out trip wires attached to hidden grenades (*above*); American soldiers would trip one of the wires and set off a grenade. In other traps, mines were dug behind logs (*below left*), or spikes hidden in the grass – which sliced through soldiers' boots (*below*).

FIELD ARTILLERY

The first field guns were used in the 14th century. They were loaded at the muzzle and were made of iron or bronze. Improvements were slow, but by the 17th century, guns were transported into battle. These guns were known as field artillery. During the 19th century, guns became more accurate and their range increased so that they could fire farther than the horizon!

NAPOLEONIC WARFARE

The French military commander Napoléon Bonaparte (1769-1821) trained as an artilleryman and understood the importance of field artillery. During the Napoleonic Wars (1793-1815, *above right*), guns were massed wheel to wheel to form huge batteries. Cannons are used today by the British Royal Horse Artillery on ceremonial occasions *(above left)*.

EARLY ARTILLERY
In the Middle Ages, the Chinese developed the first "cannons," which fired scrap metal or broken porcelain at an enemy (*above*). In the 14th century, when the simple cannon was first being used in the West, the Chinese were developing mobile battlefield artillery.

WAR BETWEEN THE STATES
Field artillery was used in the U.S. Civil War (1861-1865) by both sides – Union forces, who represented the North, and Confederates from the South (*below*). Gunners were vulnerable to rifle fire from enemy sharpshooters. The sharpshooters had rifles that were accurate at ranges of over 1,100 yards (a half mile), and sometimes they killed the entire gun crew before being spotted.

SOLID SHOT
Made from stone and then, later, iron balls, solid shot (*above*) was first used in the Middle Ages to demolish fortifications. It was also used against men at ranges of up to 3,000 yds (9,000 ft).

GRAPESHOT
Consisting of many musket balls attached to a wooden core and covered in canvas, grapeshot (*below*) was used against soldiers at close range in the 18th century. As the sacking burst, the musket balls spread out like a shotgun blast.

SHRAPNEL AND SHELLS
Shrapnel (*right*) was invented by Henry Shrapnel during the Napoleonic Wars (1793-1815). A fused iron shell was filled with gunpowder and musket balls. The shell was fired at the enemy and, when it was over their heads, the fuse would detonate, blasting the musket balls down on them. Modern shells (*far right*) mainly use the power of high explosives to harm the enemy.

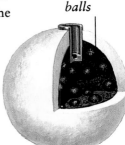

Gunpowder and musket balls

WORLD WAR II
In 1942, the German Army attacked Soviet troops in the Caucasus Mountains (*right*). Moving guns was difficult in this rocky terrain. Some armies had special mountain guns, which were broken down into separate pieces and carried on mules.

ARTILLERY TODAY
As with many other weapon systems, field artillery has become lighter and more accurate. During the Falklands Campaign (1982), the British 105mm Light Gun (*left*) was able to fire on Argentinian positions at a range of 11 miles (17.6 kilometers). It was also light enough to be carried by a helicopter. In the Gulf War (1991), the British and Americans used the fearsome Multiple Launch Rocket System (MLRS) in an artillery role. This weapon could send high-explosive warheads to a range of at least 19 miles (30 kilometers).

SIR NOEL BIRCH
During World War I, the numbers of guns increased dramatically, and thousands of artillery pieces would be employed in a major offensive. General Birch became the senior British artillery officer on the Western Front. He believed that the war would be won by having more guns (and soldiers) than Germany.

SUPER-ACCURATE
By using a laser-guided system – code named Copperhead – modern field guns can guarantee to hit an individual truck or house at ranges of well over 11,000 yds (6 miles).

THE BIG GUNS

Heavy artillery is essential for destroying enemy fortifications. There are two types. The first type have very long ranges, and are known technically as guns. The second type, called howitzers, have a shorter range but fires heavier, more destructive shells. Big guns are expensive and difficult to build, so they have only been used in small numbers.

MONS MEG
Built for use against castles in Scotland, *Mons Meg* (*above*) was the nickname of an early "super gun," which fired enormous stone cannonballs.

U.S. CIVIL WAR
During the U.S. Civil War (1861-1865), heavy guns were mounted on railroads, which made them easier to transport to the battlefield (*right*). These guns were used to smash enemy fortifications.

19TH-CENTURY DEVELOPMENTS

Improvements in engineering and in the production of high-quality steel enabled gunmakers to build larger and stronger guns. These guns withstood more powerful charges so

that cannonballs or shells went farther. Many heavy guns, such as this Krupp's 78-ton gun (*left*), were protected by being placed in forts.

WORLD WAR I
Howitzers were deployed by both Britain (*right*) and Germany in World War I to fire at targets that lay beyond the line of sight. With a range of over 5.6 miles (9 km), they were used to bombard an area before troops moved in to attack.

ALFRED KRUPP (1812-1887)
Krupp was a German steel manufacturer who designed heavy guns for his country's army. During World War I, his factory designed superheavy guns for destroying Belgian forts. Krupp's most famous gun, a 16-in (42-cm) howitzer was nicknamed "Big Bertha" after his granddaughter!

WORLD WAR II

During World War II, the Germans protected the border with France using big guns (*right*). The heaviest guns were used on the Eastern Front against the former Soviet Union (now the Russian Federation). One gun weighed 1,481 tons and could fire a 9-ton shell to a distance of over 29 miles (47 kilometers).

THE IRAQI SUPER GUN

During the Gulf War of 1991, the Iraqi Army developed this long-range super gun (*left*). It was made from long sections of tubing, which were joined together and positioned on a ramp. The Allies destroyed the gun before it could be used.

THE PARIS GUN
One of the most famous of the long-range guns was the German "Paris Gun," which was used to shell Paris during World War I. The gun was hidden in a forest and had a range of 79 miles (128 km).

BUNKER BUSTERS!
The massive 24-in (60-cm) Karl series of super mortars (*right*) was developed by the Germans in World War II to smash concrete bunkers. They were fired against the Russians in the Siege of Sevastopol in 1942, and they fired a special shell, which only exploded when it had penetrated the concrete.

ARMORED VEHICLES

Armies have needed to protect vehicles and animals from enemy attack since the earliest times. Horses, elephants, chariots, and soldiers were all shielded by armor, but wearing strong armor tended to restrict movement. In the 20th century, the internal-combustion (or motor) engine gave vehicles sufficient power to carry the heaviest armor plate: The age of armored vehicles was born.

AN EARLY TANK?
The Italian artist and inventor Leonardo da Vinci (1452-1519) produced designs of many different vehicles for the future, including this drawing of a "moving fort" (*above*). In real life, the "fort" would be far too heavy for men or animals to push.

MOBILE ATTACK
During sieges in the Middle Ages, the attackers pushed or pulled siege towers (*left*) toward castle walls. These towers provided the attackers with protection and, once one was alongside the castle, a drawbridge was lowered and troops rushed forward onto the castle walls.

TANK AMMUNITION
There are three types: APFSDS (Armor-Piercing Fin-Stabilized Discarding-Sabot) shells cut through armor; HEAT (High-Explosive Anti-Tank) ammunition forces a blast through a small hole in the armor; HESH (High-Explosive Squash-Head) shells blast fragments of armor into the inside of the tank.

ARMORED ANIMALS

Just as medieval knights went into battle wearing full plate armor (*see* pages 10-11), their horses were protected too, either with leather quilting or pieces of plate armor. The closest thing to a modern-day tank, though, was the war elephant (*right*); archers and spearmen would be protected in a fighting compartment, or "castle," positioned on the elephant's back.

TRACKED PROGRESS

The British developed the first tank during World War I – the Mark I (*left*). Early tanks could cross over trenches

British Mark I

King Tiger

and barbed wire, but had a top speed of only 3 mph (5 kmh). By World War II the tank had become a very important weapon of war, with heavy armor and a powerful gun. The German King Tiger tank (*above right*) weighed 77 tons, had a top speed of 24 mph (38 kmh), and was armed with a high-velocity 88mm gun.

ERWIN ROMMEL (1891-1944)
A German tank general in World War II, Rommel became famous for the daring way he led his troops into battle. Even his British opponents respected him, although he was defeated in the end.

ARMORED CARS
Much lighter than tanks and equipped with wheels rather than caterpillar tracks, armored cars were used for light operations. The first armored cars, such as the World War I Rolls-Royce (*left*), were ordinary road cars with armor bolted on. The American-built Boarhound (*below*) was the largest armored car of World War II. It was built for desert terrain, with powerful eight-wheel drive and a top speed of 50 mph (80 kmh).

Rolls-Royce

Boarhound

METAL MONSTER

The American M1A1 Abrams Main Battle Tank (*above*) was used in the 1991 Gulf War, and is one of the most powerful tanks in the world. It weighs 61 tons, has a top speed of 45 mph (73 kmh), and is armed with a high-velocity 120mm gun, which can destroy another tank up to 2.5 miles (4 kilometers) away.

MISSILES AND ROCKETS

BOOMERANGS DON'T ALWAYS COME BACK!
The traditional hunting boomerang of the Australian Aborigines (*above*) was cleverly designed to return to the thrower if it missed the target. However, the heavier war boomerang was designed to fly straight, and did not return to the thrower.

One of the first times a missile was used in war is recorded in the Bible, when David killed Goliath the giant using a slingshot, or catapult. Such weapons were originally developed for hunting, but their military usefulness soon became apparent. All early missile-throwing systems used the power of the human body (*above*), but the Chinese discovery of gunpowder made possible the development of rockets, which had greater power and far greater range.

Medieval European lance

Japanese yari

Roman pilum

African spear

Indian lance

Maori spear (from New Zealand)

AIR POWER
The native peoples of the Amazon region of South America use long blowpipes to hunt animals in the jungle (*right*). A poisoned dart is blown along the tube, and in skilled hands it can be very accurate.

THRUSTING AND THROWING

Spears can be thrust or thrown at an enemy, and there are many variations (*left*). The Roman pilum, for example, had a long iron point that was designed to pierce enemy shields and break off from the wooden shaft, so it could not be thrown back. This Australian aboriginal device (*right*) is attached to the end of a spear to give the user greater force when throwing.

SIEGE CATAPULTS
Invented by the ancient Romans, catapults (*left*) were also used during the Middle Ages to batter down the walls of castles. The throwing arm was attached to a thick cord and winched backward. A large stone was placed in the cup and the throwing arm was then released, hurling the rock forward.

CHINESE CRACKERS!
The first time a rocket was ever used in war is thought to have been in 1232, when Chinese troops fired gunpowder rockets at a Tartar army (from Russia). These rockets would have been like our modern firework rockets, and they were intended to frighten the enemy's horses.

WORLD WAR II ADVANCES
Rockets became effective weapons during World War II. Germany fired high-explosive warheads with a range of 4.5 miles (7 kilometers) from a multi-launch system called a Nebelwerfer. The United States and England used a hand-held antitank missile launcher (*left*) nicknamed the "bazooka" after the comic-strip character Bazooka Joe!

UP AND AWAY!
The Stinger surface-to-air missile (*right*) makes it possible for a single infantryman to shoot down low-flying jet aircraft. Developed in the 1980s for the U.S. Army, the Stinger has a range of 3 miles (5 kilometers) and can hit aircraft flying up to 3 miles (4.8 kilometers) high. After the soldier has pulled the trigger, the missile is guided to the target by an infrared homing device, which locks onto the heat produced by the aircraft's engine.

SECRET WEAPONS

Concealed weapons are useful for secret agents or for people who need to keep a sword or gun out of sight. Many secret weapons were developed for British and American agents working behind enemy lines in World War II, and they are still used by spies today. In 1978 a Bulgarian dissident writer named Georgi Markov was killed in London by a secret agent from his own country, who fired a pellet containing a lethal poison from a gun concealed in an umbrella (*right*). This illustrates the deadly reality behind fictional spy stories like "James Bond."

Trigger

Poison pellet

TIGER CLAW

The metal rings on two fingers would be the only clue that a tiger claw, or "bagh nagh" (*above*), lay hidden in a man's hand. Inspired by the ripping power of a wild beast's paw, this savage weapon was used in India in the early 19th century.

AX PISTOL

Made of steel, this highly decorated war ax has a pistol built into the ax head (*left*). Too heavy and cumbersome to be used in battle, it is most likely that such an ornate weapon was constructed for a nobleman's amusement.

GUN SHIELD

Thought to be made by an Italian gunsmith for Henry VIII, this gun shield (*right*) consists of a matchlock pistol projecting through the middle of the shield. A barred peephole allowed the shooter to look at the target while remaining protected by the shield.

GLOVE GUN
Developed for U.S. secret agents in World War II, this small pistol was riveted to the back of a glove (*left*). The agent would press his fist against the victim to set off the trigger. At such a short range the agent could not miss, and the sound from a shot is said to have been no louder than a slap on the wrist.

STEEL QUOIT
One of the favorite weapons of the Punjabi Sikhs of India was the "chakram" – a sharp-edged steel quoit worn hidden on the arm or in the turban. Once thrown, it was deadly at up to 70 yds (210 ft).

MULTI-USE PISTOL
In about 1900 a dangerous gang roamed around Paris, France, terrifying the public. They used miniature pistols (*below*) that included some secret devices: a knuckle-duster for the butt and a folding dagger on the front. The gun could only be fired at point-blank range.

PEN PISTOL
This pistol (*right*) is ingeniously hidden in the case of a Japanese writing set made about 1875. To fire the gun, a writing brush was taken out of the barrel, the inkwell lid was lifted up, and the hammer was cocked.

CUTLERY PISTOLS
These flintlock pistols (*right*) were made in Central Europe in around 1700, and were richly decorated with bronze gilt. They were built for amusement rather than for practical reasons – after all, the muzzles are pointed the "wrong way" around: directly back at the person using them.

UNDER COVER
The concealed weapons invented by "Q" in James Bond movies (*left*) are often entirely impractical. Today's concealed weapons are often made of plastic to avoid detection by metal detectors and X-ray machines at airports. These concealed weapons are smuggled by terrorist organizations and include plastic explosives such as Semtex and pistols made largely of plastic, for example the Austrian-made Glock semi-automatic.

CHARLES FRASER-SMITH
During World War II Charles Fraser-Smith worked for the British secret service, and his job was to construct special weapons for secret agents. They were highly ingenious, and usually involved concealing guns or explosives in everyday household objects like shaving brushes or pipes. He became the model for "Q" in Ian Fleming's James Bond books.

GLOSSARY

aborigine A native of Australia, whose ancestors had lived there for thousands of years before the arrival of European settlers in the 18th century.

bayonet A knifelike weapon that is fitted to the end of a rifle or musket.

Bosnian War (1992-1995) The breakup of the former communist country of Yugoslavia led to conflict in the new state of Bosnia, as Serbs, Croats, and Bosnians fought for control. The three sides were eventually persuaded to negotiate a peaceful settlement.

breech-loading A method of loading a rifle or gun at the breech (next to the handle), instead of at the muzzle (the far end).

Bronze Age A period in history when people used tools and weapons made from bronze (a mixture of the metals tin and copper). In Europe, the Bronze Age began in about 6500 B.C., and lasted until the beginning of the Iron Age, in about 1000 B.C.

chain mail A form of armor used in the Middle Ages that was made from interlocking iron rings.

Corinthian A person or soldier from the ancient Greek state of Corinth. The Corinthians developed a helmet that covered virtually the entire face.

crossbow A medieval weapon in which the bow is laid cross-wise against a wooden handle.

English Civil War (1642-1648) The conflict fought between the Royalists (or Cavaliers), who supported King Charles I, and the Parliamentarians (or Roundheads), who supported the rights of the English Parliament. The Parliamentarians won and Charles was executed.

firearms Weapons that fire bullets and can be carried by an individual. Firearms include pistols, revolvers, and rifles.

flintlock A firing mechanism invented in the 17th century. It used the sparks created by striking a flint against a piece of steel to ignite the main charge of gunpowder.

gladius The name given to a short stabbing sword used by Roman legionaries.

grenade A small explosive shell that can be thrown by an infantryman at the enemy.

Gulf War (1990-1991) After Iraqi forces invaded the neighboring country of Kuwait, an allied force led by the United States, Britain, and France was sent to the Middle East. In a short land war lasting just 100 hours, they drove the Iraqis out of Kuwait.

gunpowder An explosive chemical mixture that provided the power to fire bullets and cannonballs. It was slowly replaced in the 19th century by more powerful synthetic explosives.

halberd A spear-like weapon which is also fitted with an ax blade.

hoplite A soldier from ancient Greece who was heavily armored and equipped with a shield, a spear and a sword.

lacquer A hard, shiny, transparent covering applied to wood or metal for protection and decorative display.

lance A long, spearlike weapon used by cavalrymen.

legionary The ordinary soldier of the Roman Army who was the lowest rank in a legion, a body of soldiers which could be several thousand men strong.

longbow Used by English archers in the Middle Ages, this type of bow allowed a higher firing rate than that of crossbows.

machine gun A type of automatic firearm that fires bullets at a high rate – sometimes more than 1,000 per minute – without the need for reloading.

magazine A container holding a number of cartridges that enables a gun to shoot several bullets without the firer having to reload.

matchlock An early shoulder-held firearm, which used a lighted fuse, or match, to ignite the main charge of gunpowder.

Middle Ages A period in history stretching between the end of the Roman Empire in the fifth century and the beginning of the modern age in the late 15th century.

mortar A simple and lightweight piece of artillery used by the infantry, which throws a shell or bomb upward at a steep angle.

musket An early type of shoulder-held, smoothbore firearm. It was slow to load and inaccurate.

muzzle The far end of a barrel on any type of firearm.

Napoleonic Wars (1793-1815) A major series of wars that took its name from the great French general Napoléon Bonaparte, whose armies conquered most of Europe. Napoléon was defeated by a British-Prussian army at the Battle of Waterloo in 1815.

NATO (North Atlantic Treaty Organization) This defensive alliance was formed after World War II by European countries and the United States.

Norman A warrior people who settled in northern France and then conquered England after winning the Battle of Hastings in 1066.

pike A long spearlike weapon used by foot soldiers to repel cavalrymen.

pilum A throwing-spear used by Roman legionaries.

pistol Early handgun, which fired one shot at a time before needing to be reloaded.

plate armor A type of armor made up of iron or steel plates that was stronger than chain mail.

powder-flask A container that holds gunpowder.

revolver A type of pistol which uses a revolving cylinder to hold five or six shots that can be fired in succession.

rifle A shoulder-held firearm that has grooves cut into the barrel (rifling) which make the bullet spin. It is far more accurate than smoothbore muskets, which did not have rifling.

samurai A warrior highly trained in *bushido* – the Japanese method of warfare.

scabbard A container that holds a sword or knife.

sentry A soldier who guards a military position.

shell The case which contains the projectile and explosive charge of bullets.

shotgun A shoulder-held smoothbore firearm which normally fires many small balls – called shot – packed inside a cartridge.

siege The surrounding of a castle by an army in order to force its surrender.

Stone Age The period in history when people used tools and weapons made from stone. It was replaced by the Bronze Age which, in Europe, began in about 6500 B.C.

submachine gun A lightweight type of firearm that automatically fires small pistol bullets at great speed.

U.S. Civil War (1861-1865) The war fought between the Northern states (the Unionists) and the Southern states (the Confederates). The South was forced to surrender.

Viet Cong The name for North Vietnamese communists fighting against South Vietnam and the United States during the Vietnam War.

Vietnam War (1965-1975) Vietnam had been divided into the communist North and the non-communist South. War broke out between them and, although the South was supported by the United States, the North won and reunited Vietnam.

wheel lock A firing mechanism fitted to early pistols that was superior to the matchlock, but slower than the flintlock.

World War I (1914-1918) A large-scale conflict fought between the Allies (France, Russia, Britain, Italy, and the United States) and the Central Powers (Germany, Austria-Hungary, and Turkey). After almost five years of fighting the Allies emerged as the victors.

World War II (1939-1945) The biggest war in human history, with over 50 million casualties. The Allies (Britain, the Soviet Union, and the United States) defeated the Axis nations (Germany, Italy, and Japan).

INDEX

aborigine, Australian 26, 30
Africa 5, 9, 26
aircraft 17, 27
Alexander the Great 11
America, North 5, 15, 16, 17, 19, 25, 27, 28, 30
    South 26
archers 4, 5, 24
armor 4, 8, 9, 10-11, 24, 30, 31
armored vehicles 24- 25
arrows 4-5
artillery, field 20-21
    heavy 22-23
assault rifles 13
Assyria 4
Australia 26, 30
axes 8, 9, 10
Aztecs 8, 9, 10

battles 4, 7, 14
bayonets 7, 30
bazookas 27
Belgium 22
big guns 22-23
Bond, James 28, 29
booby traps 19
Bosnian War 18, 30
Bowie, Colonel Jim 7
bows 4-5
Britain 4, 6, 9, 13, 16, 17, 25, 27, 28, 30, 31

Cambodia 19
cannons 20, 30
castles 22, 24, 27
catapults 26, 27
cavalry 6, 10, 11, 30, 31
chain mail 10
China 9, 26, 27
Civil War, English 11
    U.S. 16, 22

Colt, Samuel 15
Congreve, Sir William 27
cowboys 12
crossbows 5

daggers 6-7
da Vinci, Leonardo 24
Dirty Harry 15
duels 7, 14

Egypt, ancient 4

fencing 7
flails 8
flintlock pistols 14, 29, 30
France 4, 6, 23, 27, 29
Fraser-Smith, Charles 29

gangsters 17
Gatling, James 16
Germany 15, 17, 22, 23, 25, 27
Greece, ancient 10, 11, 30
grenades 18, 30
Gulf War 17, 23, 25, 30
gunships 17

Hittites 8
homing devices 27
Hood, Robin 4
howitzers 22

India 5, 7, 16, 18, 26, 28
infantry 9, 18, 27, 30, 31
Iraq 23, 30

Japan 5, 6, 9, 11, 26, 29, 31

knights 8, 9, 10, 24
knives, combat 7
Krupp, Alfred 22

Lee, Bruce 9
longbows 4

machine guns 16-17, 30
Maori 26
Markov, Georgi 28
martial arts 9
matchlocks 12, 28
Maxim, Hiram 16
Middle Ages 4, 5, 6, 8, 9, 10, 11, 24, 26, 30
mines 19
missiles 26-27
mortars 18, 31
muskets 7, 12-13, 31

Napoleonic Wars 6, 27, 31
Native Americans 5
NATO 18, 31
Nepal 7
New Zealand 26
Normandy 4, 31

Oakley, Annie 13

pistols 14-15, 28, 29, 31
police 8, 9, 10
powder flasks 12
Puckle, James 16

"Q" 29

rapiers 7
revolvers 12, 14-15, 31
rifles 7, 12-13, 30, 31
rockets 26-27
Rome, ancient 6, 10, 26, 27, 30, 31
Rommel, Erwin 25
Russian Federation 23, 27

samurai 6, 9, 11
secret agents 28, 29
secret weapons 28-29
shotguns 12, 31

sieges 24, 27, 31
slingshots 26
Soviet Union *see* Russian Federation
spears 26, 30
staff weapons 8-9
Stone Age 4, 8
submachine guns 17
super guns 22, 23
swords 6-7, 10

tanks 24, 25
tommy guns 17
truncheons 8-9

Vietnam War 17, 19, ..31
Vikings 7

wheel-lock pistols 14
"Wild" West 12, 13, 14
World War I 8, 11, 15, 16, 17, 18, 22, 25, 31
World War II 15, 17, 23, 25, 27, 28, 29, 31

Picture Credits
(t=top, m=middle, b=bottom, r=right, l=left):
front cover tlt & 15m – Solution Pictures; front cover tlb & b, 4-5, 5bl, 7t, 13, 14b, 17m & b, 19 both, 21b, 23m & 27b – Frank Spooner Pictures; front cover tm both, trt & ml, 4 both, 5br, 7m, 8 both, 9m, 10mr, 20t & mr, 21m, 24b & back cover – AKG London; front cover trb, ml & mr, 10m, 14m, 14-15 & 26 both – Mary Evans Picture Library; 6, 6-7 & 9tl – Roger Vlitos; 9tr, 11, 16-17, 18m, 20ml & 24-25 – Rex Features; 12 – Denver Public Library; 15m – Warner Bros (Courtesy Kobal; 16b, 18t & 22b – Tom Donovan Military Pictures; 29 – EON/United Artists (Courtesy Kobal)